UNDER FLAG

UNDER FLAG

Myung Mi Kim

Kelsey St. Press   Berkeley, Ca. 2008

Acknowledgments:
Some of these poems first appeared in: *Calyx, Ironwood, f. (Lip),
HOW(ever), Sulfur,* ZYZZYVA

Cover art by Norine Nishimura: *Untitled Woodcut Panels Four and Five.*
Book design by Robert Rosenwasser.
Produced by Rena Rosenwasser and Patricia Dienstfrey.

NATIONAL   Publication of this book was made possible in part
ENDOWMENT   by a grant from the National Endowment for the Arts.
FOR THE ARTS

Kelsey St. Press
2824 Kelsey St.
Berkeley, CA 94705

info@kelseyst.com
http://www.kelseyst.com/

book orders: orders@spdbooks.org

for Young Ok Kim
(1922-1972)

Contents

And Sing We

Must it ring so true
So we must sing it

To span even yawning distance
And would we be near then

What would the sea be, if we were near it

                                                    Voice

It catches its underside and drags it back

What sound do we make, "n", "h", "g"

Speak and it is sound in time

Depletion replete with barraging

Slurred and taken over

Diaspora. "It is not the picture

That will save us."

All the fields fallow

The slide carousel's near burn-out and yet

Flash and one more picture of how we were to be

If we live against replication

Our scripts stricken

Black ants on tar: ponderous pending change

Fable voices, fabled voices say to us

And this breaks through unheralded —

Sardines browned to a crisp over charcoal is memory smell
elicited from nothing

Falling in that way

Um-pah, um-pah sensibility of the first grade teacher, feet firm
on the pump organ's pedals, we flap our wings, butterfly wings,
butterfly butterfly, fly over here

Once we leave a place is it there

Prattle (heard, found, made) in kitchen

No longer clinking against the sides of the pot set to boil

Prattle displaced. Guard birds

That should have been near, all along

Prattle done trattle gone just how far

Do voices carry

What we might have explored, already discovered

Falling down falling down

Callback fallback whip whippoorwill

Not the one song to rivet us trundle rondo

Not a singular song trundle rondo

What once came to us whole

In this we are again about to do

In the times it takes to   dead dead dead la la la

Trundle rondo   for a long time it stood marker and marked

Mostly, we cross bridges we did not see being built

Under Flag

Is distance. If she knows it

Casting and again casting into the pond to hook the same turtle

Beset by borders conquered, disfigured

One house can be seen

Then another thatched roof

On this side of the sea the rancor of their arrival
Where invasion occurs according to schedule

Evacuees, a singular wave set against stubbled bluffs

Rigor of those who carry households on their backs

Above: victims.
Below: Chonui, a typical Korean town. In the distance,
          a 155–mm shell has exploded.

Of elders who would have been sitting in the warmest part
of the house with comforters draped around their shoulders
peeling tangerines

Of an uncle with shrapnel burrowing into shinbone
for thirty years

A wave of much white cloth

Handful of millet, a pair of never worn shoes, one chicken
grabbed by the neck, ill-prepared for carrying,
carrying through

Not to have seen it yet inheriting it

Drilled at the core for mineral yield and this, once depleted,
never to be replaced

At dawn the next morning, firing his machine gun, Corporal Leonard H.
was shot and instantly killed while stopping the Reds' last attempts
to overrun and take the hilltop

The demoralized ROK troops disappeared but the handful of Americans,
completely surrounded, held out for seven hours against continuous
attack, until all ammunition was exhausted

General D.'s skillful direction of the fight was fully as memorable
as his heroic personal participation with pistol and bazooka

Grumman F9F
Bell H-130s
Shooting Stars
Flying Cheetahs

They could handle them if they would only use the weapons we have
given them properly, said Colonel Wright

Lockheed F-04 Starfire
Lockheed F-803
Bell H-13 Sioux
Bell H-13 Ds

More kept coming. More fell

Is distance. If she could know it

Citizens to the streets marching

Their demands lettered in blood

The leader counters them

With gas meant to thwart any crowd's ambition

And they must scatter, white cloths over their faces

Every month on the 15th, there is an air raid drill sometime during
the day, lasting approximately 15 minutes. When the siren goes off,
everyone must get off the streets. An all clear siren marks the
end of the drill.

And how long practice how long drill to subvert what borders are

What must we call each other if we meet there

Brother sister neighbor lover   go unsaid what we are

Tens of thousands of names

Go unsaid the family name

Sun, an affliction hitting white

Retinue of figures dwindling to size

The eye won't be appeased

His name stitched on his school uniform, flame

Flame around what will fall as ash

Kerosene soaked skin housing what will burn

Fierce tenement of protest

Faces spread in a field

On the breeze what might be azaleas in full bloom

Composed of many lengths of bone

Food, Shelter, Clothing

And of isolation, rock salt, jars preserving

Oxen returning on paths they themselves have shaped

Line of vision heeding lines of hills stretching

Farther west, farther east, than one had thought

Along the meadow

The wanderer's gypsum shoes

Crossings and bearings

Steadily pernicious

She could not talk without first looking at others' mouths (which language?)

(pushed into) crevice a bluegill might lodge in

They had oared to cross the ocean

And where had they come to

These bearers of a homeland

Those landing amphibious (under cover of night)

In a gangplank thud and amplification take

Spot of ground. Fended it might remain

Republic and anthem, spot and same spot

How little space they take up given the land's reach

All those whose feet had resounded

Smear fear tyranny of attack

Already the villages already the cities receding

A face hauled away and a small flag of the country nearby

They were stripped

They were made to roll in one direction then the other

If they didn't do it right, they were kicked

An ambulance on which the words "blood bank car"

Had been written in blood

It is this plastic around our heads

Whenever we enter the streets

That peppery smell meant to deter

And this plastic over our heads

These men these women are throwing stones

These men these women chant and chant

"In my country" preface to the immigrant's fallow

Field my country ash in water follow

Descent   slur   vowel

Stricken buoys

Span no tongue and mouth

Scripting, hand flat against the mouth

Up against bounty and figured human

        allaying surge

                   neighboring

Geographical trodden shelter

Locate deciphering

           by force

As contour

Hurls

     ga ga ga ga

Will be plain foil credo

Figures pervious arboretum

                ave   mella   ferro

Into Such Assembly

1.

Can you read and write English? Yes_____. No_____.
Write down the following sentences in English as I dictate them.
     There is a dog in the road.
     It is raining.
Do you renounce allegiance to any other country but this?
Now tell me, who is the president of the United States?
You will all stand now. Raise your right hands.

Cable car rides over swan flecked ponds
Red lacquer chests in our slateblue house
Chrysanthemums trailing bloom after bloom
Ivory, russet, pale yellow petals crushed
Between fingers, that green smell, if jade would smell
So-Sah's thatched roofs shading miso hung to dry —
Sweet potatoes grow on the rock choked side of the mountain
The other, the pine wet green side of the mountain
Hides a lush clearing where we picnic and sing:
     Sung-Bul-Sah, geep eun bahm ae

Neither, neither

Who is mother tongue, who is father country?

2.

Do they have trees in Korea? Do the children eat out of garbage cans?

We had a dalmation
We rode the train on weekends from Seoul to So-Sah where we grew grapes

We ate on the patio surrounded by dahlias

Over there, ass is cheap — those girls live to make you happy

Over there, we had a slateblue house with a flat roof where
I made many snowmen, over there

No, "th", "th", put your tongue against the roof of your mouth,
lean slightly against the back of the top teeth, then bring your
bottom teeth up to barely touch your tongue and breathe out, and
you should feel the tongue vibrating, "th", "th", look in the mirror,
that's better

And with distance traveled, as part of it

How often when it rains here does it rain there?

One gives over to a language and then

What was given, given over?

3.

This rain eats into most anything

        And when we had been scattered over the face of the earth
        We could not speak to one another

The creek rises, the rain-fed current rises

        Color given up, sap given up
        Weeds branches groves what they make as one

This rain gouging already gouged valleys
And they fill, fill, flow over

        What gives way losing gulch, mesa, peak, state, nation

Land, ocean dissolving
The continent and the peninsula, the peninsula and the continent
Of one piece sweeping

One table laden with one crumb
Every mouthful off a spoon whole

Each drop strewn into such assembly

Arrival Which Is Not An Arrival

1.

Right hand traced over and over in thick white crayon

The fatigue of the birthday girl who has wrapped cheap
but brilliant ballerina pins, favors for her guests

What, all over, is the same?

Squirrels forage for nuts. Then scratch in attics.

Slack-mouth look of infants

A child shirking back knows the hand is slap

Tall trees waving the way they shouldn't if they are that tall

How did anything happen?
How does anything happen?
Many things happened.

2.

He comes home singing quail, quail me

Infinity of a declaration

In parts clean in parts dirty

A coal oven, ominous biscuit baking

In parts clean in parts dirty

Rivers course through oceans like rivers on land

Which is colder, ocean or river?

Study anatomy, course of our blood and its arrival

Pasted on a wooden bench, avowal of pity, piety in a sunbaked
brick chapel, picture of a picture book Jesus baby

Adoration for holding adoration for light we did not see
We, mother and father to what we must be rid of

There was no ceremony. After, we ate at that place
under the 125th St. stop

And the mother held their heads under and none
splashed and they floated, assured, down

3.

The world poses as an unbearable fruit

A slanted chair in a narrow room to de-emphasize the elongated room she

Grief pooling is the same all over

Sturgeon thick into body middle thickening thinning

Valiant children on a ship bound by blood scrub crimson health

Of symmetry, of repose
to hear repeated light, tree, blue
the child mouth opening first, first

The world beckons with corporeal promise, blood and its dwelling

Flour sack of glutinous possibilities fruiting

Flour plaster coils demure body

Body As One As History

Weight of breasts or milk and all blood

This is a tree. It bears fruit.

Ministering to body filling no munificence

This is the body feigning. It is large as I.

Time rage, churn of one part and another

Nothing to succor what is dense and fragile at the same time

Inaudible collapse

Given the body's size, size for a grave

Pallid pellucid jar head

Gurgling stomach sack

Polyps, cysts, hemorrhages, dribbly discharges, fish stink

Skin, registering bruise or touch

But the body streaked black across a red brick wall

The body large as I, larger

Save the water from rinsing rice for sleek hair
This is what the young women are told, then they're told
Cut off this hair that cedar combs combed
Empty straw sacks and hide under them
Enemy soldiers are approaching, are near

And in this way she tried to keep them alive — two dried anchovies
for each child and none for herself. The train gathering speed. And
with no words but a thrust of a fist holding out money the soldiers
stroke their penises cup their balls, push stripped plastic dolls
with black ink scratched on between the hard twig legs into her face.

Treadle needle tread thread. Left armhole, right bodice. Cotton
rayon nylon dust. The crouch of the mother over machine over
a child's winter coat over a stream rinsing diapers
when night falls while the soldiers ranged while the border loomed
and she crossed it. Over a blouse 3 cents over a skirt 5 cents and
in this way

This is the body and we live it. Large as I. Large as

Tips of their fingers touching or not. Women on a clover field where
brown rabbits have just fed. Rise of line of women stretching to the
rise of land. No one moves. Every muscle moves. No one approaches.
In their mouths, more than breath more than each sound buzzed inside
the inside of the mouth.

As large as.

Demarcation

Widest angle of vision before vision fails to mean

Where circle returns predator and prey

Prefaced earth's face

Turns to broadcast scarce cover of dirt

Between this and next

Afterbirth of the first child planted with

Planted with a sapling the now full swerving pine

And that same child scattering a last handful of dirt

For send-off, for delineation

No trace on earth of what is said

No way to put a palm up against it

The treble, the trouble, of woods, of words

Elements. Elemental. So speak. Air water rise fall

No way to speak it

Larynx thin string, strung

Unschooled pulley throat

A bird calls out in perfect thirds: do-mi, do-mi

Domi, domi, saal zsin domi
Domi, domi, oh fat snapper   As complicated as it is

As dirt is scrubbed off that a thousand hands smear on

As dim railings pen children at long tables spooning gruel

As the infant face is absence onto which we say
     It is like — it is like —

As a compass locates relocates and cuts fresh figures

As silence to mate(d) world

Not founded by mother or father

Spun into coherence (cohere)

Cohere who can say

These Fishing One

More than one fears

More than one buries

The renege of forerunners who return

Nothing to teach   years of stoops swept and rinsed

In these orderly houses

Late late I must a

Ribula fibula mae disparaging did pass and passed along

What is this place

These Fishing Two

Born earlier and what would have been tropic, polar

Under or over water, pushed apart by what kind of time

A walk in the dark (dark)

A walk to seal

That it was sealed

Hung towels, blankets, artifacts left for shield

It was one city then another in quick succession

These Fishing Three

In what place streets best known, earliest nickname known

Ah, her child face (as she remembers it)

Ah, her child face (as the photograph of it replaces the memory of it)

These Fishing Four

Here, the thermos shattered

Here, the well and we drank, drank

Here, the snake and the family side-stepped it

Here, the dress worn once and torn

Here, perch and sheephead weight the line

These Fishing Five

The seal of a difficult year born and slid away

Articles of clothing given away piece by piece

Fft-fft spitting out seeds not to be had

Granaries will be wrecked

Welts in marble inured to injury

These Fishing Six

As soldiers of this great enterprise

Perforce the intrepidly stationed buoys

Whose names lingering

What one thread to bring next to needle eye

From The Sea On To The Land

Field from which all the dancers have gone

They've chosen me, the one without   to stay

Let me and let me

That flowing, how could it just be water

This I'm pointing to, without roots vines or leaves

Nearer to year and year

Only this, only there's more

House built one palm's reach at a time

The wickedly steeping clock
Wickedly a thing I know

Diminuendo for what passes

To bear   to bear

Descant for feeble contractions

                              Aviary   ovary

Downward cast   Plot of land staked with twigs and twine
For homes, the leaders assured

For their counterparts a head taller muscles fuller vocabulary better
they fatten the cows bind the fruit trees to deliver marbled meat
luscious fruit and themselves sit down to boiled millet and an
onion or two pulled out of the ground

Many historic secular buildings were also damaged

The natives they brought with them for service, being naked
and in chains, had perished in great part during the winter

Children masquerade as their elders and are pleased
The elders plant azaleas and dogwoods where they were
in the yards of the elders before them

Wretched repetition worn

For long, forlorn, have I desired

In a world to be reapportioned beginning (that) day

Ribboned (recognition) superfluous

Discomfiture of (walls)

Disaster in (milliseconds) effortless

Scourging does idiocy (pass)

To take the scene of (shame) and embroider

(Upahead) vision version nor bees neither honey